the walks

We have created **two unique Walks** in Lancaster, which can be enjoyed separately, or joined together to form one longer walk - depending upon available time and energy! Both have been carefully chosen to highlight aspects of the city which might otherwise remain hidden.

1. Castle To Dalton Square

Wind your way round the commanding John O' Gaunt's castle, nestling alongside Lancaster Priory, before descending rapidly into the centre of the city. Walk along a 12th century street and through Lancaster's coffee quarter, before exiting Market Square – the beating heart of the city. Out now to the languid canal, overlooked by Lancaster Cathedral, before finishing at Dalton Square, centuries old and steeped in history.

2. Dalton Square to River Lune

From Lancaster's historic Dalton Square this walk runs along vibrant but ancient lanes and streets, where modern meets the past. Explore Market Square with its museums, and places where people can sit, talk, listen and watch. Read about Lancaster's fascinating past as you make your way to its imposing castle, set on a hill. Down now to finish your walk at the River Lune, once home to Britain's fourth largest port.

1

Instructions

First walk

Read page 4 initially, which provides a useful overview. Then follow the route which is described on the bottom half of pages 5 to 7, which should be used in conjunction with the route map that you'll find on pages 8 and 9.

The top half of pages 5 to 7 contains interesting information about one or two historical features you'll encounter on the walk.

For those doing the Treasure Hunt, you'll find clues on the bottom half of pages 5 to 7, which relate to the set of directions. The very first clue is usually at the start location, or very close to it.

Sometimes the clue asks you to identify which of the pictures, on the bottom half of page 4, matches what you can see – your answer will be the letter relating to the picture.

Write your answers down on page 13. If you're having difficulty finding the answer to a clue, page 14 provides further help. Page 16 contains the answers.

Second Walk

Read page 10 initially, and then continue with pages 11 and 12 in the same way as above.

Directions

LHS   =   Left Hand Side
RHS   =   Right Hand Side

Safety

Users of any Curious About Walk are solely responsible for the safety of themselves and their party whilst completing the walks. We cannot be held responsible for any loss or damage to property, or accident or injury to life and limb incurred whilst on a Curious About Walk.

Further general safety information can be found on our website under FAQs, and any specific advice relating to these particular walks can be found on pages 4 and 10.

We hope you have an enjoyable journey of discovery! Stay curious...

History of Lancaster

Lancaster, Lancashire's county town, dates back at least as long ago as the Roman occupation, though little remains of that time.

The city's name was first recorded in the Domesday Book in 1086 as Loncastre – "Lon" referring to the river Lune, and "castre" from the Roman fort which stood there.

A Saxon church was later built within the ruined Roman walls as Lancaster became a strategic trading centre – by medieval times ships were using the River Lune. A castle, perched high above the river defended the town from attack and provided the focus for the dispensing of local justice. For a short while Lancaster became the fourth most important port in the UK's Slave Trade. Its legacy of fabulous Georgian architecture gives the town its character today.

Lancaster has unique ties to the British Monarchy - the house of Lancaster was a branch of the English royal family, whilst the Duchy of Lancaster holds large estates on behalf of the Queen (who herself is the Duke of Lancaster).

The traditional emblem for the House of Lancaster is a red rose (the Red Rose of Lancaster), similar to that of the House of York which is a white rose. Rival claims to the throne erupted into civil war during the Wars of the Roses. In more recent times this rivalry has continued in sports between Lancashire and Yorkshire, including the Roses Tournament in which Lancaster and York universities compete every year.

Lancaster was granted city status in 1937, and today has a population of over 50,000.

Castle to Dalton Square

Start:	4 Hillside (see map), LA1 1YH
End:	Centre of Dalton Square, LA1 1PN
Distance:	1.5 miles, 2.4 kms
Time:	1.5 hours
Take Extra Care:	
Accessibility:	Steps down from The Priory can be avoided using the detour marked on the map. No clues are missed. Several of the streets have cobbles which can be uneven at times.
On the Way:	Near the start The Storey Arts Centre (G on map) is worth a visit. Close to The Priory (H) are the remains of a Roman Bath (I). The city Museum (J) in Market Square is worth spending some time in. Lancaster Cathedral (K) is near the end of the first walk. Throughout the walk the Ashton Memorial in Williamson Park (L) can be seen above the city. This is worth visiting if you have the time. You will pass many shops, pubs, cafés and restaurants on this walk.

Picture Matches

The following pictures have been taken along the two routes. Match the picture letter (no sequence implied) to each of the clues marked

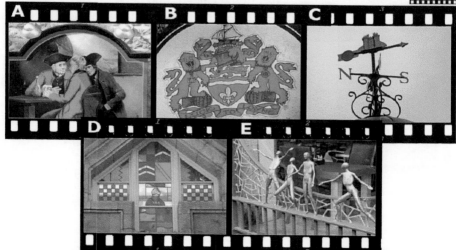

4

Castle to Dalton Square

Lancaster Castle (A on map), is a medieval castle, whose beginnings date back to Roman times. Occupying a commanding position on a hill overlooking the town of Lancaster and the River Lune, it was a bastion against the invading forces of the Picts and Scots tribes. In 1164 the castle came under royal control – today it is still owned by the Duchy of Lancaster (The Queen is Duke of Lancaster). After Scottish invasions in 1322 and 1389, there was no further military action until the English Civil War. The Castle was first used as a prison in 1196, until it was closed in 2011. The castle has witnessed 200 executions from murder to witchcraft to stealing cattle – earning Lancaster its gruesome nickname – The Hanging Town. One example is Father Edmund Arrowsmith who said Mass locally. For this 'crime' he was arrested in 1628 and subsequently hung, drawn and quartered, and the parts of his body exposed on top of John O' Gaunt's Gateway. The last execution took place in 1910.

From #4 Hillside, walk towards the city (see map). Turn left at the end on Long Marsh Lane and continue along the right hand side of Castle Park.	1. At the start, which philosopher was born March 26th 1911?
	2. Picture Match?
	3. When did Paley and Austin start business?
Left at the end on Castle Hill, keeping right. First left up a footpath towards the Castle and cross a small road towards the Castle entrance. Continue along the footpath around the Castle to The Priory entrance (no clues). Walk alongside The Priory, then down steps. Turn right along St Mary's Parade, then Castle Hill, keeping left.	4. Looking up above doors, what did Shrigley & Hunt make?
	5. At a corner, if the crowd was huge, what was the rope?
	6. Looking left, Alex Stevens designed which aqueduct?
	7. What did the dispensary provide?

Castle to Dalton Square

The Music Room (B) in Sun Street dates back to 1730 - built as a garden pavilion, not for listening to music! Its name is probably a corruption of 'Muses Room' as the 9 Muses decorate its walls.
Eventually the Music Room's garden was sold for development and by the end of the 18th century the garden had disappeared. In the 19th century it was turned into a factory, and it was only in the 1970s that the Room was bought and lovingly restored as holiday accommodation above and a shop below.

Market St & Market Square (C) have probably existed since 1193 when a charter was created to allow Lancaster the right to hold markets. The Police and Fire Stations were situated in a corner of the Square and prior to 1782 there was a market cross, near where the fountain stands today.
Lancaster City Museum occupies the Old Town Hall, which dates back to 1783, showcasing the history and archaeology of the city, as well as being home to the King's Own Royal Regiment Museum.

Left at the end on Market Street, keeping right. Cross the main road ahead, and continue along Market Street. Take the 1st left up Sun Street (Music Room Passage). Continue along Sun Street keeping right. First right on Church Street, then next right on New Street, keeping right.	8. When did they give you bride cake?
	9. Picture Match?
	10. At a corner, who created a map of Lancaster in 1610?
	11. Looking left, up high at a corner, Picture Match?
Left at the end on Market Street, keeping right. Near the end of Market Square, turn right into Marketgate. Turn left at the end on Cornmarket then James Lane. Turn right at the end on Penny Street.	12. Which corner is linked with Market Square in 2014?
	13. Looking right, at a corner by benches, when is the Time Capsule to be opened?
	14. What was 'likely the first Roman road north through Lancaster'?

Castle to Dalton Square

In 1612 twelve **'Pendle Witches'** were arrested for witchcraft and the murder of ten others.
The story probably began with an argument between one of the accused, Alizon Device, and a pedlar, John Law. Alizon asked John for some pins - he refused and Alizon cursed him. Shortly afterwards John Law suffered a stroke, for which he blamed Alizon and her powers. Subsequently Alizon confessed that she had told the Devil to lame John Law. Upon further questioning Alizon accused others of witchcraft, and the trial was set in motion.

During the trial the 9 year old daughter of one of the accused stated that she believed her mother had been a witch for 3 or 4 years. She also said her mother knew someone who appeared in the shape of a brown dog, and who had been asked to help with various murders

Of those who were tried, one was acquitted, one died in custody, and ten were found guilty and executed by hanging at Gallows Hill in Lancaster.

Take the next left along Brock Street, keeping right. Straight over Thurnham Street along Dalton Square then Nelson Street, keeping right. Cross over the canal and turn left along St Peter's Road, keeping left.	15. Looking right and back at a corner, which word did Richard Owen invent?
	16. Looking left, Our Lady Queen of where?
	17. Looking back at the canal, name of the 1876 bridge?
Take the next left over the canal and along Moor Lane, keeping right. Turn left at the end of the Golden Lion pub, up Bryer Street, keeping right. Right at the end on Sulyard Street, keeping right. Left at the end to the centre of Dalton Square ahead (via the middle entrance), where your first walk ends.	18. Looking back, whose College is Mill Hall?
	19. Which witch was Mother Demdike?
	20. Looking up at a corner, who was Mayor, Nov.27;1873?
	21. Who is below Leighton Turner and Ruskin Millais?

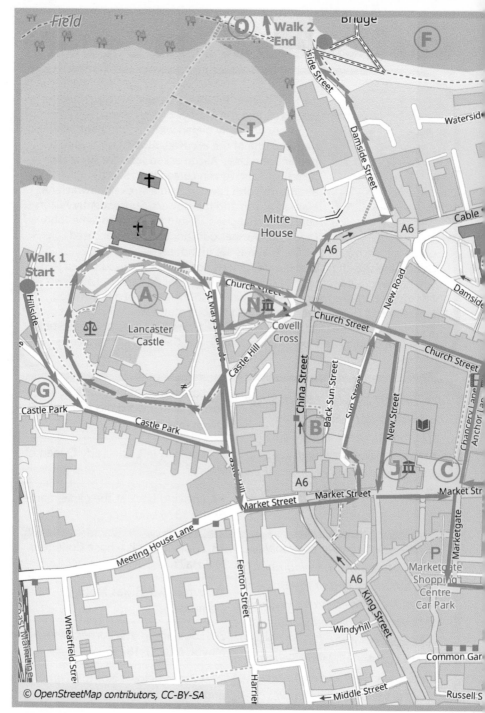

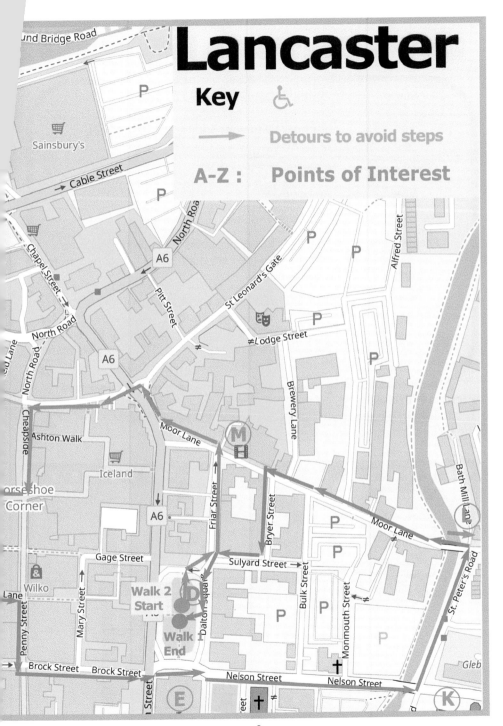

Lancaster

Key   ♿

→   Detours to avoid steps

A-Z :   **Points of Interest**

Dalton Square to River Lune

Start:	Centre of Dalton Square, LA1 1PN
End:	Start of Millennium Bridge, Damside Street, LA1 1AH
Distance:	0.8 miles, 1.3 kms
Time:	An hour
Take Extra Care:	Alongside the River Lune at the end.
Accessibility:	There are uneven cobbles on Church Street and Nip Hill, and they are quite steep - see the map for a diversion.
On the Way:	Near the start of the walks The Dukes Theatre (M on map). The Judges Lodgings Museum (N) on Nip Hill and the Maritime Museum (O) near the end of the walk, are both worth a visit. You will pass many shops, pubs, cafés and restaurants on this walk.

Picture Matches

The following pictures have been taken along the two routes. Match the picture letter (no sequence implied) to each of the clues marked

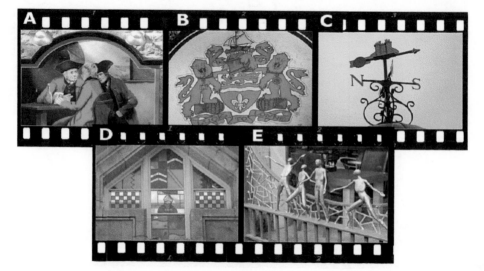

Dalton Square to River Lune

Dalton Square (D on map) occupies the site of a Dominican Friary which was sold to Sir Thomas Holcroft at dissolution in 1539 and a house called the Frierage built (now number 18). The Square was redesigned in Edwardian times.
The Victoria Monument boasts a statue of Queen Victoria and four bronze lions - the panels have reliefs of eminent Victorians, including Lancaster-born Florence Nightingale.

The new **Town Hall** (E) was designed by E W Mountford, who also designed the Old Bailey in London. Palatine Hall was originally a Catholic chapel, before becoming the Hippodrome variety hall and opera house, and then the County Cinema, and now council offices. Next to it is number 2, the home of Dr. Buck Ruxton who killed his wife and maid in 1935 and dissected and butchered them both, wrapping their remains in newspapers. He then drove to a remote Scottish location where he disposed of the 'packages', but a few days later was apprehended by the police, tried, convicted and finally hung!

From the centre of Dalton Square proceed down Friar Street, keeping right (see map). Left at the end on Moor Lane, keeping right.	22. Looking up at the start, who gave to his native town in 1906?
	23. Who was a Knight of the Royal Prussian Order?
	24. Looking up at a corner, who invented the Railway Ticket Dating Press?
Right at the end, then first left up Church Street, keeping left. Next left up Cheapside, then next right along Market Street. Next right at Market Square, keeping right, and ahead down Anchor Lane.	25. At a corner, what was St Leonard's named after?
	26. At a corner, where is it said that "the grasshopper eats only the finest leaves"?
	27. Looking left and up, at a corner, Picture Match?
	28. When was Bonnie Prince Charlie proclaimed Regent?

Dalton Square to River Lune

In the 18th century the port of Lancaster, on the **River Lune (F)**, was the scene of an extensive and profitable trade with Africa and the Americas as part of the slave trade. Between 1750 and 1775 Lancaster ships made 100 voyages to the African coast (typically The Gambia and Sierra Leone), and carried almost 30,000 slaves to the West Indies and South Carolina. By 1780 Lancaster ranked as England's fourth largest colonial port after London, Liverpool and Bristol.

In return for the slaves Lancaster would import slave-produced sugar and rum as well as mahogany to supply the town's thriving cabinet-making industry. It wasn't until 1790 that the slave trading finally stopped out of Lancaster.

In addition to slaves Lancaster also exported a variety of goods to the plantations in the Americas, including fine clothing, beef and furniture, as well as knitted caps, salted fish and work implements for the slaves. At home, colonial imports encouraged sugar refining.

Left at the end on Church Street, keeping right. Continue over the A6 and straight ahead up Nip Hill. Right at the end then next right down Church Street keeping left.	29. Looking up as you turn, what does Church Street mark through Roman Lancaster?
	30. Who lodged in Mrs Livesey's House?
	31. After whom is Covell's Cross named?
	32. Near this spot stood the East Gate of what?
Left at the next crossroads down Bridge Lane (no clues). Next left along Damside Street, keeping right until you reach the start of the pedestrian bridge over the River Lune, where your second walk ends.	33. Looking left & back, Picture Match?
	34. To the right, what's between cotton and mahogany?
	35. When was the medieval bridge first mentioned?

Your Answers

Castle to Dalton Square	
1.	19.
2.	20.
3.	21.
4.	**Dalton Square to River Lune**
5.	22.
6.	23.
7.	24.
8	25.
9.	26.
10.	27.
11.	28.
12.	29.
13.	30.
14.	31.
15.	32.
16.	33.
17.	34.
18.	35.

Where's the Answer?

1. Castle to Dalton Square

1. Plaque on #4, RHS Hillside
2. Sign at the end of Long Marsh Lane on LHS
3. Plaque on #24, RHS Castle Park
4. Plaque on #23, RHS Castle Hill
5. Inscription on white stone, start of the footpath from Castle Hill
6. Plaque on The Priory
7. Plaque on #19, LHS Castle Hill
8. Plaque on the Royal King's Arms Hotel, RHS Market Street
9. Sun Café, RHS Sun Street, opposite #26
10. Information board at the corner of Church Street with New Street
11. Top of the last building, LHS New Street
12. Information board RHS Market Street at the entrance to Marketgate
13. Plaque at the end of Marketgate, on RHS
14. Information board at the corner of Penny Street with Brock Street
15. Information board at the corner of Brock Street with Thurnham St
16. Plaque on a building, LHS Nelson Street, just after Bulk Street
17. Sign on Nelson Street Bridge, above the canal
18. Sign outside Mill Hall, RHS Moor Lane
19. Plaque on Golden Lion pub, RHS Moor Lane, opposite Bryer Street
20. Inscription on Wesley House, RHS Sulyard Street, corner with Bryer Street
21. Inscription on Queen Victoria Statue, centre of Dalton Square

2. Dalton Square to River Lune

22. Inscription on Queen Victoria Statue, centre of Dalton Square
23. Plaque on #7, RHS Friar Street
24. Plaque at the end of Moor Lane on RHS
25. Information board at the start of Church Street on LHS
26. Information board, LHS Church Street, start of Cheapside
27. Above the entrance to St Nics, end of Cheapside on LHS
28. Plaque, RHS Market Square, just before Anchor Lane
29. Plaque on Banks Lyon, RHS Church Street, end of Anchor Lane
30. Plaque on #76, RHS Church Street
31. Information board just after crossing the A6
32. Plaque on Mitre House (Job Centre), LHS Church Street
33. The Three Mariners pub sign, LHS Damside Street
34. Captured Africans 'sculpture' RHS Damside Street
35. New Bridge information board under a bridge, by River Lune